Sand Dancer

and other poems

Also by Wendy Wright

Gooseberries, Urchin Books

Fingertips, Urchin Books an interactive (V.A.K.) learning programme for the acquisition of reading and writing skills for early years and special needs children

"Letter from a Survivor" was awarded a Highly Commended in the Segora Open Poetry Competition 2011 competition and also appears in the accompanying anthology.

Sand Dancer
and other poems

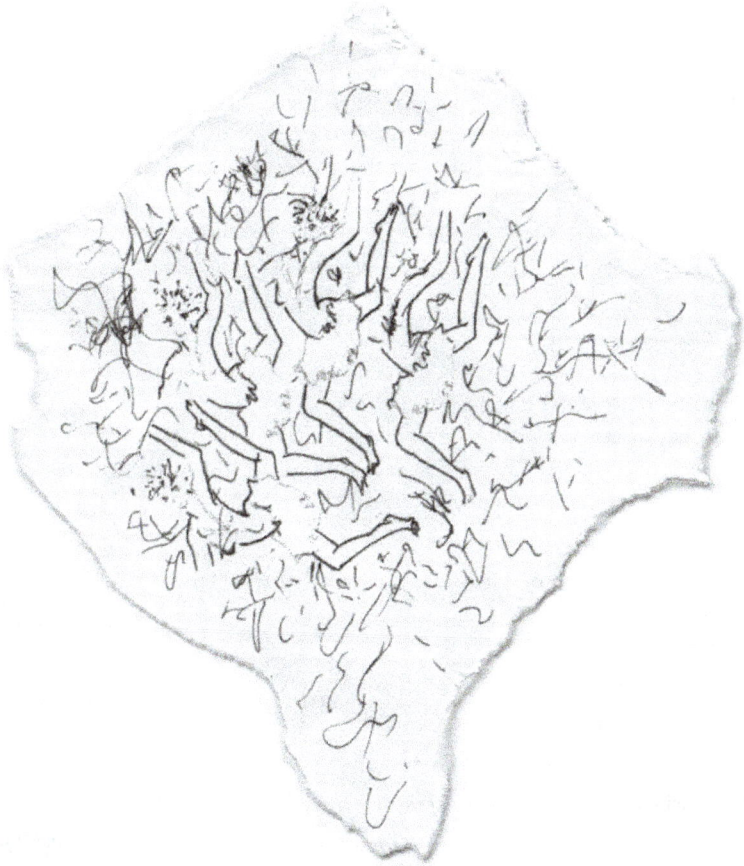

Wendy Wright

First printed in this edition 2012
Perigord Press, part of GunBoss Books,
3rd Floor, 207 Regent Street,
London, W1B 3HH, England
www.perigordpress.com

ISBN 978-0-9561581-6-1

Photograph and artwork credits

Photo on "Sand Dancer"
This work includes the photo "Merce Cunningham April 16, 1919- July 26, 2009", available
under a Creative Commons Attribution license, © Floor.

Photo on "Schama, Bernini and me"
This work includes the photo "Extasis of St. Theresa", available under a Creative Commons
Attribution license, © Sailko.

"Improvisation 31"
Reproduction of Wassily Kandinsky's painting *Improvisation 31* by kind permission of the
National Gallery in Washington, D.C.

Photos on "Vimy":
This work includes the photo "Vimy, Pas de Calais, France", available under a Creative
Commons Attribution license, © isamiga76 and the photo "Railway Dugouts cemetery one",
available under a Creative Commons Attribution license, © Redvers.

"The Designer"
Reproduction of *Self-portrait by Durer as a young man* by kind permission of the Prado

All other artwork is by Wendy Wright, including the cover image, *Sand Dancer*.

Dedicated to Ivor Meggido,
dancer, teacher, choreographer

Acknowledgements

Special thanks to Brenda Walker and Gordon and Jocelyn Simms for their encouragement and guidance.

Contents

A note from the author

Not all of the poems in this book are directly about dance, but they have all been influenced by my deepest inner sense of the rhythm, pattern and movement in life, with its constant changes and surprises.

By the age of four I found myself trundled off to boarding school, where we had – joy of joys – ballet lessons! For two hours every Saturday we bounced and shuffled our precious ballet shoes on a dusty wooden floor.

In religious silence, our hair scraped back to near baldness, we entered another world of 'the dance'. We were supplicants in a temple of wonderful music and trained to master our unruly bodies. There were lots of things I was not good at – but I was fine in anything to do with two legs or two hands – and took me off the floor. Added to the dance lessons were gymnastics and acrobatics led by an ex-army physical training instructor.

I was learning to fly.

Dance had released me from the floor and helped me to play with gravity, and the space around – to become whatever I liked, to change time, seasons, my age, my size. Soon I could hear music and rhythm everywhere. In my own breathing and heartbeat, everything rising and falling, speeding up and slowing down. Nothing was ever still.

A lot of language tumbles over you in a dance class stressing and supporting movement and exercise, or the particular mood and emotion of a dance or story. So rhythm in single words, rhyming words and phrases of language became entwined with the power of repetition and patterns of movement that over time impressed itself upon me as poetry.

During this process, on a deeper level of consciousness a certain philosophy had taken root in my life. I had been taught to understand I was part of something enormous, outside of my self and that nothing begins and nothing ends. All of life is moving and our relationship to all living things on earth is how we sense eternity.

W. W.

April 2012

Merce Cunningham

Sand Dancer

On the death of Merce Cunningham

There is dust on my feet
from dancing in the car park,
sticking to my toes,
beige grey, sandy
gritty, pitting my heels
reminding me
dust made the world.

The spinning top of whipped up energy
sparked the earth and made me,
so the volcano is under my feet,
its eruptions the light behind my eyes
and dance is whooping to get out...
A cadenza of tapping, finger-snapping,
free-wheeling –
endless inner music – serpentine –
the start of time, it pulls and
tugs at my ears...

Ruled by the Big Bang.
At the beginning of the world
a fiery beat fired bullets
still reverberating – undercover –
bouncing off the walls of my veins;
ping, ping, ping,
fire – recoil,
movement – repose.

Inside my skin another skin
waiting on wings,
full of wisps and pirouettes
of falling leaves –
sputs and spurts –
frisson from bacon frying
and showers of arrows
leaving pinpricks for
trails of blood music and
empty bellies, bulging eyes
rootling about like fluttering
moths turning to dust.

I am only this dance.
I am only this dust.

Even my thoughts
turn cartwheels then
stamp their feet to castanets.
Falling – clapping –
flying,
not to land eventually,
there is no landfall.
Dust is swept into patterns –
blown, changing form,
one day a river bed
another a child.

The quick and the dead
all dance forever
to the rhythm of the rising sun.

Tango de Noche

The night has a secret.
Set free from the stare of daylight
a half-open tiger's-eye of a moon
looks down on its own creation.

The Pampero is blowing in cigarette
smoke from treeless-plains,
unfastening the raven hair
of night to fall on shoulders
of enfolding scrub. Pomaded,
percanta-warm – shadow's
arms entwined.

That rustle is time stirring
in some cantina.
That sigh is lips-brushing footwork,
intricately criss-crossing
waterless ground,
leaving no trace of past or present.

The living and the dead fused
into one shape reflected
in smouldering lakes,
lit by a melody of stars –
lilting to the ears of the
lost and the dispossessed.
Longing briefly re-defined.

Napoletano

You have a certain wisdom I rely on,
carefully I try to fathom where it comes from,
but stand bewildered with my ball of thread,
for there are no labyrinths to find.

Words are pennies sliding through your fingers,
ideas appear like eggs from up
your sleeves and behind my ears.
Like a child you have me tirelessly
grinning, delighted by your tricks.

You are behind me and ahead of me
at the same time –
arriving at a finish line
before I have started.
You have answers before I have
questions – all combined in
the Commedia del Arte of your mind,
making me restless
for what is coming next.

In this bright arcade of shining windows
am I looking at you or is it
reflections of you that I chase?
Then from nowhere you
whirl me round…

I have become accessory.
Without me the whistling
Catherine Wheel of your soul
would be boxed-in.

When I slipped my arm through yours
I won a jackpot of language,
riches in a currency
only few can spend.

For so many, words are
not only worthless,
they are also an offence.

*Napoletano is the local language spoken in Naples and
the Sorrentine Peninsular.*

Gnena

Danced upon the day and chanted,
drumming on the heels of the wild sky
and the young men dived
in a laughing wave
spun from a curve of joy.
Shining, young – lapped in play
a galaxy of spray –
curls shaken
into nowhere-far-enough-to run away.
Reflections ricochet one day
into a thousand days
that burst around the sun.
I cover my eyes.

Across the years such brightness
leaves you marked and grazed.

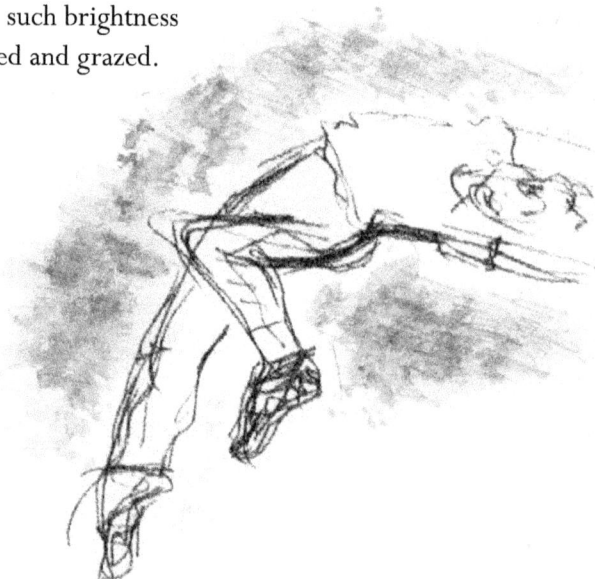

Remembering Serena Grimaldi, Malta 1970-1972

White Wedding

You can smell snow,
even from far away,
it's promise tingles in
the stillness of the air.

Behind the sky's closed eyes
snow flakes vie to pattern
bridal paths and wedding veils,
as the wind tunes up
its pipes and drums.

Soft kisses and bright halos are
slipping under covers –
feathery, ever- spreading sheets
and counterpanes.
White – white, full of lilies
sheaves and garlands.
Ermine night gowns petrified,
laid out for a wedding night.

As icy patches thicken
and ruts are hidden
turn over in your sleep –
reach out – for
under the deadening flattery
of snow lies marriage…

Fauré Pavanne

Europe is waltzing,
circling and whirling.
Polkas are panting,
breathing hard, out of breath –
galloping sweating horses,
to the rhythm
of canons, gunfire and war.
And Fauré is writing a Pavanne,
for the plaintive pipe of
the Midi Pyrénées.

The High Renaissance
steps and steps, side by side,
soft footfalls cushioning hard floors,
and the Pavanne breathes out.
A sideways glance at the simplest form,
it turns and turns – tick-tock
to the pattern of the clock,
as one day follows another
in an unbroken line of life,

and the ancient chain dance
flowers from growing
revolution, politics and war.
Delicate, clinging unseen
hardly heard.
Wistful reassurance
of life quietly taking a breath.

A Big Boy

He enters the room with gale force
and attacks his books.

It's difficult to get him to look at me
and he's always slightly
out of breath.
"I've finished this......
It's nearly the end!"
The great race to the last page,
to be able to say – "I've done it!'
To gloat and preen to his mates.

He has about half a dozen coherent
phrases of his own – his own language,
the rest is kick and punch.

But here in my room, it is a world apart –
separate – the door is closed.
The big boy can smile at the giant in
the story – he can run his fingers over
the pictures – the flowers,
the snow – the rain.
"You're doing really well," I say
"You're getting to be such a big boy now."

His eyes slide under his arms,
he's almost out of the door,
he mutters to the wall,
"But I wish I was a little boy."

Remembering Jamie

The Burning Fields

The volcano is smoking its head off –
no one sits at its right hand,
it glowers above spindly lean streets.

Somewhere – deep underground, is
a gathering inferno of passion.
Even the sea's heart beats
to the rhythm of its desire.

Cobweb spray is dripping blue
from voracious waves
that sacrifice my gaze,
dashing it on eager rocks –
replete, satisfied, they sidle
to the belly of the deep.

It is not an act of faith,
no one asks you to believe,
only the sky writes its own visions.
I rub my nose against that sky,
a man films some islands
on the horizon – it is tribute
then he leaves.

While we walk the burning fields
anxious, clodhopping –
filled with expectation,
our flimsy lives
no match for this
yawning landscape
that rounds on me
open-mouthed.

And all the Gods and all the sons of Gods
won't change a thing...

Schama, Bernini and Me
(a thing goin' on)

No one writes odes to joy any more,
but somewhere between the ironing
and the washing up, a voice
put its arm around my shoulder
and led me away.
His words – finely cut –
strung a diadem inside my head.
It was again a shining bright morning
of childhood.

I will tell you tales you have not
heard before.
I will take you to places you have
never been before.
Not to trudge down rancid streets –
I skipped from churches
to palaces, my ear to doors and
windows learning the whispers,
the gossip, of scandalous lives.
Smiling together at antics, politics,
and tactics of long ago,
that had left us with this marble treasure
of Santa Theresa.

No longer cold stone,
her waxy silken flesh now warm
with sweat and soft moans
at the peak of absolute release –
of total joy.

When the world turns without you,
in that space between the universes
of your spirit and your body.
I was caressed by this voice,
by the words, beguiled by
two men at the same time.
Like good wishes circling
candles on a cake,
questions shone out –
of what they knew?
What they knew of each other?
What they knew of me?

They seemed
to tell their own story,
of those who never meet, but
whose soft words cherish and fulfil
more surely than a lover,
in the mysterious union that springs
from the beauty of perfection.
I put the crocs away.
A thoughtfully arranged pattern
on the shelf, glinting in the spotlight,
poised- ready- awake.

Transverberazione…
I don't know this word
But I know what it means.

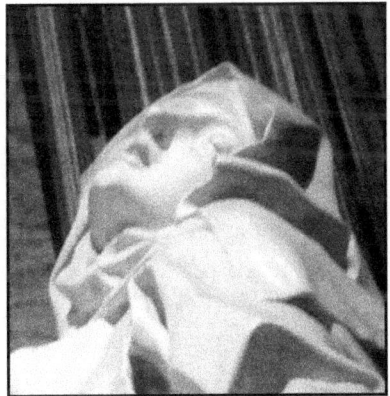

Detail of The Ecstasy of St. Theresa
by Gianlorenzo Bernini (1652)

The Gardens of Campania

Careful not to drink the water
of the eternal pool of sea and sky,
I lingered in the lost world of your eyes.
In cloisters of canopied pines,
melon flowers and lemon trees
whose siren-perfumed shadows
filled my veins…

I breathed in your opium.
You are tap rooted in these gardens,
fed from a well-spring of legend,
your tendrils grip wild rocks and stones.

I slipped from my skin,
garlanded by your honeysuckle,
with jasmine and columbine clinging,
intertwined with shocks of purple
Bougainvillea curls tumbling from high
granite walls – burgling olive groves,
running wild – exuberant in deep ravines.

I have plunged into the sea of Ulysses.
That yearning fragrance,
carried on the breeze, is you and I,
lost sailors marooned forever
in your siren gardens of Campania.

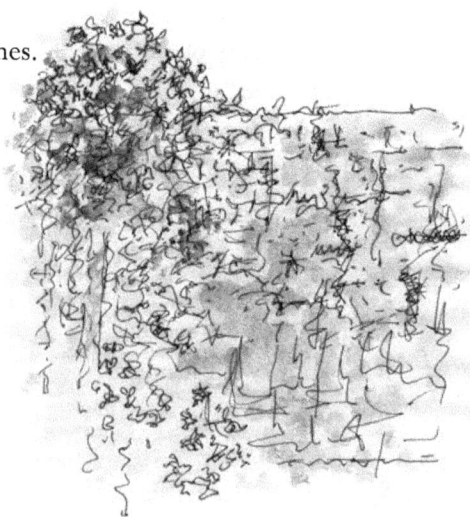

Dawn – Corfu

A slow dawn unravelled the
last threads of night.
Bright needles pricked fissures
in the hills and re-traced
the contours of the island.

Rose-blue dipped and cornered
narrow tracks,
settling behind flat roofs,
windmills and church bells,
picking out the edges of
the valleys and slipping unseen
into the sea.

It spun on and on, yard by yard
into a seamless cape and small trees,
their boughs scrubbed golden,
signposted this transubstantial phase.

Fugitive

Today the Sirocco is blowing,
barnstorming its way
around the city,
kicking in my doors
with studded desert boots.
Gate-crashing the lives of strangers,
covered in gritty beige dust –
a camouflage of sand and sweat
air-lifted from the Sahara.

Shutters clatter for help,
locks rattle in answering
gun-fire – raising Cain.
Inner doors fly open,
an assault of bad temper
and bad feeling is swearing at me.
Holed up in my retreat
I am over-run.

Across a thousand miles
this tantrum rages.
Stamping its feet – everything flying –
shouting – demanding my attention.
Hold tight to the mirrors.
Bolt the doors.

Then I see doves lining
the branches of the tree below
and red roofs high above.
I have been betrayed.

Racing headlong from room to room,
in this wind-rush of delirium
I am complicit.
Wars end – times change,
but some disfigurements
never leave you.

What Love Is

In you I see my own reflection.
Through my mirrored glasses
our wide-open eyes speak,
taking depth-charged sonar
readings.

We have colonised an underworld
of cocooned compassion
and radiating from its core
of white heat is a pollinated
landscape of space, distance
and pure air,
tingling with discovery.

Response to the song I Want to Know What Love Is *written and performed by Foreigner*

A Long Wait at the Narai

Death plucks at your sleeve,
smiles at you through the eyes
of the Thais, in shops and offices
in cafes and on the streets.
Death is very special here.

Bangkok coughs its lungs up
into air that is no longer air,
but a choking mould – spawning
until it fills every channel,
every space, every pore.

You can see it settling in layers,
on the buildings furred and diseased;
on horizons sticky with opaque
poisonous shawls of blurred
pre-destination.

Dawns and sunsets grease
a pathway for sunlight
that sometimes burns through,
but mostly burns out before
giving up the struggle
and by midday rests behind
tired fume filled lakes
re-fuelled by the morning's carburettors.

Thoughts from a hospital bed in Bangkok

Letter from a Survivor

I have lived in a time of horror.
For another's dream, everything
I loved was taken from me.
Choked by ashes and cinders –
left face down.

So I chose simple beauty
to be my life-long companion.
Cutting into the world,
laying out a thousand pieces.
New threads, sewn into a new
pattern left me by my love.

All rage spent...
blood crimson, proud gold,
ambitious veridian set aside.
Instead, a silver organza sky and
dusty purple from heather-capped
hills where we walked.
Aqua blue, my tears, my questions
rising and flowing watering
a cratered landscape.

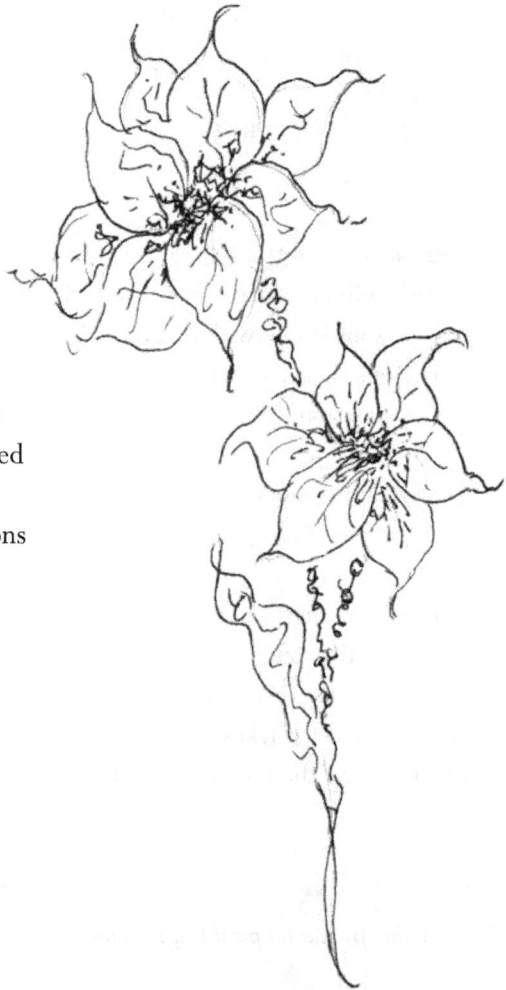

"Look for the wild flowers",
he said, in the mushroom-clouded
wasted desolation —
and ragged and unkempt they crept
like the sweet softness of his lips.

A promise kept...
Disordered hope — fragile among
the daisies and forget-me-nots.

I roughly trace my slight stitches
into skeleton chains strewn across
the small canvas of my life
holding tightly to hope —
the parterre, the pathway,
for only after hope comes faith.

A poem inspired by a panel of embroidery
Fleurs D'Azure *by Michiko Nomura*

Disdain

When did the last bride walk through
the gates of the Villa Pompeiana?

On large round tables still,
are damask cloths
now patterned by dust.
Ornate iron chairs
sprawl across a floor
of dead leaves, snuffling
at their clawed feet.

Greying columns
untidy, unattended,
frame a wistful grandeur
of sky and sea and
two thousand years of history
cross the palm of my hand.

Where do the brides go
now they have deserted
such splendour?

This colonnaded terrazza
on cliffs overlooking the bay
is elegantly withering.
its beauty redundant,
its delicacy fading
and nature's bailiffs are moving in.

In the town and along the Peninsular
the population boils over –
bubbling and sizzling among
squawking traffic.
Plasticky shop windows of purple and green
and harsh steel mirrors are trying hard
in an uneasy truce with old stones,
but high wedge-heeled gold trainers
win the day.

I slink back to the hilltop,
decaying and decrepit –
to the Villa Pompeiana where I belong.
A siren call goes out from
the big ship in the bay –
it waits...

Vesuvius leans on its side and shrugs
smirking at the sky, snorting
'How little you know...'

My feet slip unsteady
on the broken steps and uneven flagstones
that still bear the weight of wonder and disdain.

Improvisation 31

The Flying Dutchman has his
maps, tackle and charts
stowed inside the vortex
stretching to infinity,
held in by nets of
longtitude and latitude.
Framed in a square it becomes
a Rubik's cube, its colours
moving and changing.
It will take eternity
before the pattern will emerge.
Sky all around,
slowly moving out of the sun,
opposing elements and forces
in an unending battle of wills.
An improvisation that plays
at containment.

A poem in response to
Improvisation 31
(Sea Battle), 1913
by Wassily Kandinsky

A History Of The World

On the spread of your shoulders
I watch a history of the world unfold.

Gods become men.
In sacred groves nymphs wait…

…and Pan's pipes —
just out of reach,
on the tuft of a breeze,
while away a drowsy afternoon.

Narcissus smiles at his own
reflection,
his black curls ruffled by time.

In his eyes night falls.
Phoenicians, Moors and pirates
raid —
swords sticky with blood and
violation.

Lords rise and press their clammy
hands full of priapic ash
upon the heads of farmers,
fishermen and mothers
washing clothes.

Wild Strawberries

After midnight it was cool until dawn,
when skeins of sunlight
washed the dew-laid grass
and rinsed the roses
bright as cats eyes.

Around my feet, scrambling
across bare earth
a ragged swirl of tangled berries
their ruffled leaves, gypsy skirts,
lifting in the breeze and mocking
up-turned wild strawberries,
rough skinned.
Ruby red babies lips puckered for a kiss.

The men had stood by their machines
frowning in satisfaction,
leaving a wounded land.

Crazed earth had baked all summer
and stayed ignored,
only rain softened
its bewildered stare;
until stalks of grass bent their backs
against the whip of winter,
and the pity of frost coated the land.

Barely a sigh brought the balm of snow,
a soft shawl of respite
where forgotten small things lay low
under the leaves and bracken.

Like so many small things tucked away
in the back of the mind
– seeds –
tiny fists embedded in the ground;
ideas escaping from some
house of correction.
Tenacious, defiant, unrecognised,
wilfully scratching a name
on our lives.

Bowls-full of wild strawberries
fill my mouth,
I taste their sweet patience on my tongue,
the pips still sticking in my teeth.

For Jan

Resurrection

Looking inside the eye of Paradise
I can see time has settled on us
like dust.

Layered and ringed by years,
we are figures buried upright,
face to face, palms touching.
Artefacts found in the wrong
place, the wrong millennia.

Lit from within, our silhouettes
of unconquered wonderment
are fiery on the skyline of
the next world.

A revelation, much discussed
then casually overlooked.

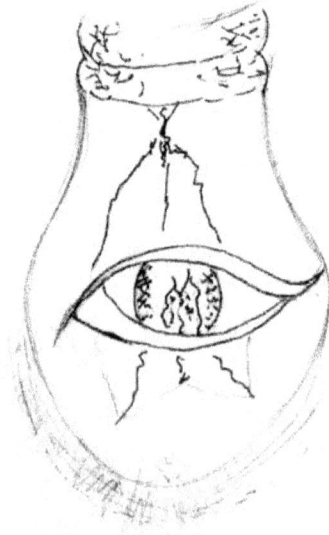

Naples Chiaroscuro

Naples, Napoli…
It pouts and lisps,
hangs around the tongue and lips,
but Naples is the bad guy
indifferent to its smoking gun,
hinting at pomaded hair and
small moustaches.

In mirrored sunglasses it
comes at you dry eyed,
rough tongued – where
smiles are not free
and eyes are catacombs leading only
to a city seething with madness.

A few crowded boulevards,
mostly sly souk streets
where the clutter of existence
wakes each day to find it still there.
Long past even remembering to want
outstretched arms – wide open lungs.

Castel Nuovo, marooned by uproarious traffic
stampeding down from the corniche,
its bugle horns keeping us in our place.
The Palace of the Bourbons wisely
stands foursquare, its back to the sea –
to the bay of various blue, keeping its
own counsel, its distance, its legend.

Naples buckles under its own weight.
Passed from hand to hand with centuries
of ignoring its masters, preferring
resentment and occasional rebellion.

In the after-life of Naples
only the dogs lie still on hot cobbles
in attitudes of quiet death.
Dawn comes and the past rises from its grave,
in winding sheets, mired in the confusion
of festivals, festas, black shirts
and yankee doodle.
The immense Catholic accumulation
serving both blood and superstition,
untiring, keeping it all alive.
There is no death in Naples.

Magnificent – Munificent – Eternal,
where every day is the day of the dead.
Their fingers signing up to new whims,
mouths virtuous and smiling
at the signores of misrule who
spawn misery and persecution.
Lords temporal and spiritual
apparently looking the other way
feasting on sacrificial lambs.

Beggars materialise – insistent
pecking crows on corn –
more, more, caw, caw…
A small boy, eyes pecked to blank sockets
holds us hostage….
accusing, demanding….
'Panini, Panini,'
a few euros is not enough.

In the safety of a Bank – a
baroque cathedral of nightmare,
standing before a Caravaggio –
his own face soon to die –
eyes cloaked – pale –
the pallor of a southern city's
greyish ochre, like the boy,
burned from a black background.

Naples, my lifted stone, is
crawling out from under vicious
truths that bite like mangy dogs
racing to the boat knowing
they will be beaten back to meet themselves.
After everlasting change of ways and means
we recognise this city –
we have lived here many times
and behind the eyes everything
stays the same,
with its own alluring smell of sweetness
and decay. Virility and vitality –
spume from spray-canned stones
that spit at you.

Infidelity

Keeping to the shadows
of guarded conversation –
avoiding bright lights,
Sorrento takes me back.
Opens its arms,
kisses both cheeks
puts an arm around my shoulder,
but, shrill and pestering
Naples has me careering
from the station
to the port.
Promiscuous in its tastes,
mysterious slaps across the face.

I hang around street corners
searching for my phone.

Vimy

I can't remember who was on the throne
in the first world war.

The voices of the poets
and posters with pointing fingers elide
with old films and sepia photos.
Men with dirty faces, are looking at me.
They are tired and mud-soaked with
'lucifers to light their fags'.

Standing here on the now grassy places
where these men were
a belligerent silence bellows.
Those millions wiped the smile
off the faces of kings.

For every blade of grass
across this plain
a man's voice was lost
and another found.

Outrage has been billowing for decades.
it's dusty groundswell still settling
on bodies piled high with dead ideas.

So don't take my photograph,
don't write my name.
There is no dignity in our
discord and dismay –
where every poppy is of a different kind.

It is an insidious peace
that has crawled all over us,
where war has flourished,

but our right to bicker
in our armchairs has been won
and visions from stumps of peace
that may one day bloom.

For those men
our rough and ready cheer,
we are still here.

Going back to that ridge,
looking out at a new landscape
of hills and valleys,
woods and streams
as far as the eye can see...

It is that ever lengthening boom
of silence that I hear.

A Homecoming

Not the same sun,
composed – following the line
of the polished river.
Its hard stare attentive only
to its shiny silver buttons.

A homecoming on roads
lined with resolute trees –
not the same roads

Not the same sun,
with no shadows.
Through bare trees,
a shiver of anxious leaves.

A wide-eyed sky
blue with fear, straining
over the road's arms,
feeling around for
a rhythm, a greeting,
one last try to please.
Valleys rigid their clipped
wings veering away,
no longer swaddled
by landscape.

Beyond — behind
a stiletto-sharp clarity
of mirrored edges
teetering inwards,
to suit truth's nail bitten smile.

Sitting straight —
looking to the front,
biting into a break-your-teeth day.

Sending Me Your Sun

Against my face your warm cheek nuzzles,
you are sending me your sun,
nosing around my neck –
closing my eyelids.

Fingers tip-toe across my lips,
hands cup my chin – hold my gaze,
tilt my face to kiss away cold years
as ice caps melt in my eyes and
bruises ripen on my mouth.

Your sun colours and defines me,
leaving your imprint
and in every line and in
every smile – forever
you will be clearly seen.

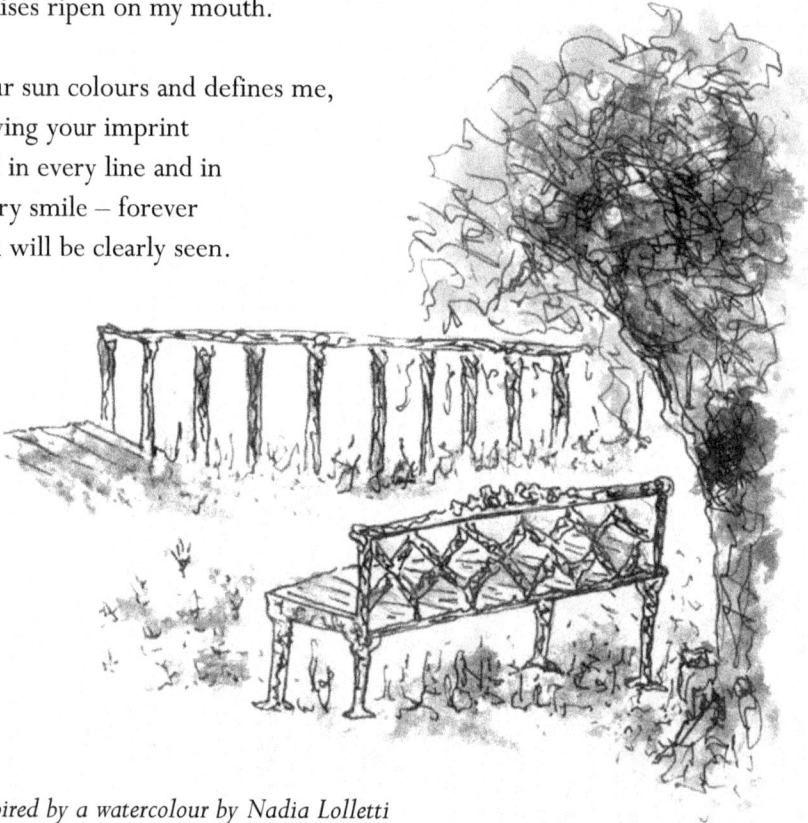

Inspired by a watercolour by Nadia Lolletti

The Designer

I am another man not made from
clay or stone,
but from a silken cap found
a desert's distance from creation.

I am the designer.
Setting the looking glasses,
arranging the candle light to
frame my skin where
tendril-falls of hair embrace
the surface to dream warmth.

A thick cord yokes my drowsy gown,
but for you all breathing particles
can be seen blindfold.
For the first time to truly
see yourself and
feel the beat of another heart
Singing within your own.

Self-portrait by Durer
as a young man

Nowhere Wars – A Rap

Boys fight wars and die
smiling on mantle pieces.
Men have to live in the half-man
place, not home – rearranged,
medals weighing them down
from the nowhere wars,

and its slow to glory,
only in small back rooms
and on anniversaries,
wheeled out, uniforms
crisply pressed,
eyes sliding sideways
who is still here?

The legends won and warm
are held aloft in drink
and sloughed off yearly
until threadbare.

Sounds dim in the blur
of brand new pyrotechnics;
worn out memories fade,
surrounded by fresh
uncomprehending faces.
Sitting in waiting rooms
new preoccupations fill the
space you hobble round.
It is no matter.

The day, the hour
it rings again.
Spin the bottle
who will it be?
Who's turn this day?
A child runs across
a playground
it can be them,
they may be marked

Guns scream like gulls...
'We're coming, we're coming...'
hiding behind a bush
and fashions change and kitchens
are refitted...
"Oh yes, I heard... tragic".
Stalked by dead men
their elbows nudging,
battle dressed –
patrolling streets mine-filled
with feral youth and giggling girls
and women you can't touch –
anxious if they will touch you.
Behind the lines
seeking kinship.
above, around, those blind
bones – their voices...
carrion caws...
in the nowhere wars.

Keeping Company

Mr Allardyce — a name for
lairds and lords that races
down the valley and rises to
the tops of the hills.

Mr Pick — in a too tight
suit, one finger-tapping
at the keys of his computer,
while he answers the phone
about tax enquiries.

Donall is his hair — fields of
clover-curls, shot through with
a cauldron of setting sun —
radiant on the District and Circle
line sashaying home to South London.

Nana's warm-as-treacle pudding
Ghanaian vowels rumble tumble
across continents, reverberating into
a heartbeat of laughter, pumping
fresh blood across the arteries of a city.

Ladies in school offices — wicked
laughter behind glass windows
their Morse Code on killer heels
'giving it large' on dreary grey days.

Cat-walk elegant and reed slim,
a gas man who came to read
the meter and stayed on
for "cakes and ale" laced
with crackling conversation.

In the half-here/half-there
of my sick room a cast of thousands
decorate my walls. Waiting
for buses, sitting in traffic and
ordering drinks in the pub,
folded and pressed between
lost pages – unexpectedly pristine
and as the tide rolls in and
threatens to cover me, I shall
not go down alone.

Making and Doing

What I do is me.
What I say is for you
to die away. Its echoes a
swan song for daylight,
a buzzing of bees dead by
the next night.
You will find me in the
making, encumbered,
harvesting, picking at chaff –
curious,
insistently smoothing already
flat-as-a-board sheets.

Altered state

I can smell the lemons and
the melons of your skin.
I rub the leaves between my fingers
and breathe you deeply in.

Hot summer nights crowd through
windows and open doors.
The avenue of trees is waltzing
in your sticky heat,
an invitation to cheek to cheek,
nose to mouth, arms to waist,
hips to thighs.

Awash in your fresh
honeydew made flesh,
my gown of heart-shaped lilac leaves
has your heart-beating presence
enmeshed into its seams
and playfulness exudes
from its pantheistic weave.

No powder, crosses, needles
needed here.
It is transubstantiation…
I sniff the leaves and we are one.

When Cicadas Sing

In the sultry painted night
when cicadas sing,
the stickiness of day sweats
sap from bark and leaves —
a pot-pourri of memory
around my neck.
I turn and turn — my own
thurifer, throwing off
covers of airless darkness,
each precious breath
filling my lungs, my heart,
my head.

Drawing you in again and
again,
as the sun rinses the sky
clean of its own blood,
leaving me to thirst
for your warm blood —
and fever-sharpened
fingernails of arousal claw
at my inside like knives.

*Response to the poem 'Harmonie du Soir'
from* Les Fleurs du Mal *by Baudelaire*

Handwriting

When I remember I hide my hands
for they hide nothing.

When I forget –
I grasp the air and poke and jab
and burst it with my fist.

Like you, I carve great angel's wings
around my phrases
and the shapes and patterns
from my fingers
make pictures of the words,
framing them for you to hold,

And when I take your hand
I find them
red pencilled into the tracery
of your palm.
My words gouged life size
on milestones
marking out territory,
sign-posting the heart and the head,
criss-crossing the lifeline's
meeting points.

You close your hand and
put it in your pocket.
I hide mine behind my back.

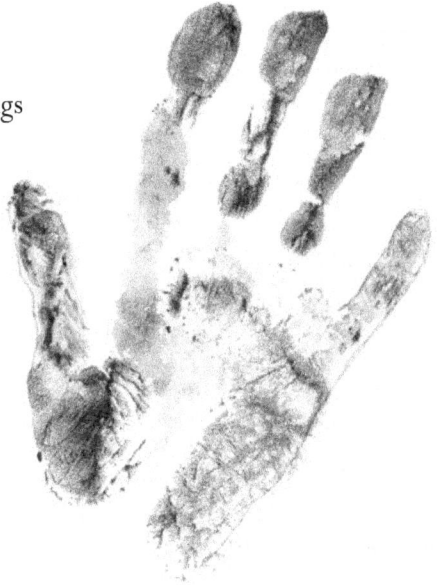

Ballet Girls (of Degas)

Dancers take to the stage
weightless – spectral in
sea-spray skirts. Child-brides
their firefly leaps
catching the light,
catching the eye,
moving phrases poised
in clear geometry.

Their names and faces left
behind, they submit to the
tyranny of the ballet.
In the wings and rehearsal
rooms – their heads
together – they murmur
slumped on benches,
fretting over satin shoes,
waist bands and tired bones,
their brilliance stolen.

Watched by men – top-hatted,
cravatted and spatted
calculating which one takes
their fancy.
Their prey the downy limbed
petal-fresh young bodies,
supple, pliant – lips geisha-red,
gracefully settling into their roles,
trained to follow the rules in silence.

Seventeen

Drenched in perfume
in a dress of dusty azure
agonised over in Oxford Street.
Does it make me look too pure?
Do my breasts show through
just enough?
Does it show off my back and my
shoulders?
Do my hips roll when I move?
Do my earrings make my eyes sparkle?
Does my lipstick shine in the dark?
Does my skin feel like a rose petal?
And is my hair inviting to touch?

Arranged at the dance floors edges
he approaches – I don't look round
led masterfully on to the dance floor
squeezed into an embrace like a vine
Hmmph!
The trouble with men is there's
only one thing on their minds!!!

Late fifties teens! Seventeen in 1957.

Looking at Nudes

There is a figure in the Matisse Museum
on Cimiez hill.
Nutmeg brown – a man from the Levant.
Life size he stands, his head forward
over a striding leg,
looking out at the marble villa's
wide halls, light corridors and airy
rooms filled with masterpieces.
Slabs of dense colour – wedge shapes
and lucid, pure, load bearing lines
take you forwards and backwards –
in every direction beyond our own time.

The man from the Levant
is looking at you
he is looking at his future –
for you are the same.
Separated by two thousand years –
you are the same,
body, height, hands, feet –
shoulders too wide for your frame.
and both of you are the Blue Bathers,
the charcoal nudes, Les Danseuses Creoles
you share the same breath,
and I can smell these people
feel their living flesh.

Lying together under the trees
I ponder…
"Wonder what that ancient Greek
would think of us?"
"He'd think it was time for lunch!"

Without You

If summer comes and goes
without you and storms
fly kites too high for
for me to chase;
windblown and unkempt,
whistle-through-your-
teeth-days pile up
like leaves against a fence.

Looking for winter
dusty moths and flies,
unsure in sun and heat
turn to gaudy russet –
kept waiting.

Looking for winter
taking light breaths –
nothing deep.
Turning with the clock,
not knowing which
way to face.

Looking for winter
missing what is overtaking
on the inside.
East and west is lost,
the sun sets early
and clouds are still
in a stopped world –
too heavy to push.

Diaspora

As day ambles into evening
sometimes I can hear
my mother laughing.

We go on
like book-ends enunciating clearly
to cover a distance of
sequences of thought
and disparate lives.
Lost –
without ransom,
left with planning and schemes.

Fixed dates and times
are lobbed across dinner tables,
and wincing voices trickle
out of bathrooms
caught –
missing the connections.

Amalfi Coast Chain Dance

They are still there the Gods
who rule our lives and
barter with our destinies.
They are still there and
sometimes you can see them
in the wind that carved the gusts
and billows of this coast road
from granite-faced rebellious
lions of the sea;
their manes of spruce and
fir braced, bent double
against an ancient power.

Campanella blooms and vines
are folded around jagged
ears, closed and impassive to
tales of conquest, war and death
and capricious Gods throwing dice
for human lives.
Rounding the headland is the
golden fleece of the sea,
out of reach. It glistens,
oiled with sailor's sweat
in a lullaby of autumn sun.

It is a disappearing act tantalising
travellers into believing a chimera
of mysteries – for by the next
conca azzurra it is gone –
they are done with it.

Changelings — now whirling
demons, tearing the coat from
your back, snatching bags and
tugging at fist-fulls of hair.

Patient umbrella pines, under a
cellophane sky are watchful,
beside flimsy Saracen Towers —
once stores of hope that crumbled
long ago — and in the
high walled towns, where sunlight
slices its way through tiny streets,
we accept this meddling and adapt.

Those eyes of dreams and madness
follow us down the years — watch us
circle — our arms linked and
as one vision is snatched away
we change direction, moving
from one high point to another.

Finding You

Finding you in the empty spaces
where the words run out
in the lees of the will.

Finding you in old clothes —
that cul-de-sac of wilted dreams,
wafer-thin once deceived,
their night duty put aside.

Finding you in the smell of bread
and in smiles up-ended —
pitched forward — as light
rain halos around your head
and some ancient banishment
whirlpools — no longer derelict.

N.C.O.

I went down with you,
dismembered across a Scottish hillside.
I look into the glass mountain,
and see myself glaciated,
tiny and stiff.

The wind swings in —
wayward —
and I am here moon-fenced.
A child dwarfed by these ruins.
Shifting particles
forming, re-forming,
lit – paltry,
revived by dawn.

An echo bounds and re-bounds
on old head stones,
winking, playful, edgy.
I pick at scabs so they wont heal.

In memory of my father

IN REMEMBRANCE

A "potted history" of the Author

Born a week before World War II was declared, Wendy's father enlisted in the RAF in 1939, before joining Bomber Command. Her mother moved back to Walthamstow, east London to stay with her mother's parents. Living in an area with industry and essential services gave her family front row seats for the Blitz; Wendy celebrated her first birthday in the garden bomb shelter. Wendy's father was killed in 1942 and her grandfather, an A.R.P. Warden, died the same year. By V.E. Day, there were only women left in their house.

Wendy was sent to Elms Boarding School before she was five and remained there until she was eleven, when she passed the scholarship to the Walthamstow Grammar School for girls. Virtually raised by her handsome, volatile and temperamental eastern European grandmother during holidays – her mother was a vague and pleasant figure, but had her own work, life and friends. Her grandmother was very talented, singing, playing the piano, acting and dancing, and deeply frustrated by the life she led. This made their relationship difficult and complex, but her influence on Wendy's career was powerful. By the time Wendy was sixteen, her mother had re-married and moved away.

Dancing and acting were a major part of Wendy's childhood. While at the Elms, she studied with a Russian-trained ballet dancer who recommended she audition at Sadlers Wells. Her acting began with the Deanery Drama Group, continuing at the newly founded Greek Theatre Players in Walthamstow, when her adorably eccentric English teacher gave her the role of Cordelia in King Lear.

A typical teenager of the 'rock and roll years', Wendy rebelled. From a call box at the end of the road she phoned for a small van to transport her and her possessions to her surprised mother's doorstep. She lived with her mother and stepfather until she married Jim Wright at the age of twenty-two. At the age of nineteen, Wendy had met Jim during a production of Trojan Women — he played a Greek soldier in a fetching leather mini-skirt, with Wendy as Helen of Troy.

Wendy acquired her L.G.S.M. (Licentiate of the Guildhall School of Music and Drama) in 1963, shortly after her eldest son was born. Being involved in many productions, she regularly attended drama courses and on one of these met Ivor Meggido, a professional dancer, teacher and choreographer. Wendy attended his jazz dance classes for years, describing him as "the most amazing man who gave me to me."

Jim took a post teaching at Tal Handaq Naval School in Malta at the end of the sixties. With two sons in tow, they let out their house, packed up car and kids and travelled to Malta –a fantastic time for all the family!

While there, they joined the Malta Amateur Dramatic Club, or MADC, who mounted productions at the Manoel theatre in Valletta. An acting master class for Wendy, as many of the 'sixpenny settlers' were ex-theatre pros. One man had produced Ealing Comedies and another the former Head of Drama for Jamaica T.V. They stripped Wendy of bad acting habits and provided a phenomenal experience, allowing her to be involved in productions and musical choreography. Wendy also ran a dance group at the Sacred Heart School as well as a cabaret group for the Maltese. Heaven!

Upon returning to the UK, Wendy got her teaching qualification from Avery Hill College in Mile End (affectionately known as 'Fag End'), gaining a distinction and joint top of her year in English Literature — it would have been a scandal if she hadn't after all those years of experience studying drama and poetry!

Wendy became a primary school teacher at Barclay School, in Waltham Forest, taking to it like a duck to water, very quickly taking charge of dance, drama and gymnastic groups. This included collaborations with the music teachers to produce huge school concerts with more than three hundred children.

In the meantime one of her former Drama lecturers, Brenda Walker, approached Wendy for support. Brenda had travelled with UNESCO behind the Iron Curtain into Eastern Europe in the eighties before founding an international publishing company, Forest Books, to publish their work. Wendy describes working with Brenda as being "like living in a high wind where stout oaks tremble and deck chairs fly out to sea." It was an astonishing time and they did a great many things together, including attending the World Congress of Poets in Bangkok where Wendy managed to contract malaria!

A change of career took her from the classroom to Special Needs Teaching, involving more training, research and "very interesting courses" at Queen Charlotte's Hospital. Continuing research with the assistance of many children, Wendy developed a comprehensive teaching system for language development and the full range of reading and writing skills called Fingertips. Inspired by Brenda, Wendy and Jim started a small publishing company called Urchin Books they used to publish the materials for the system. As Jim had taken early retirement, they proceeded to exhibit and give talks, workshops and lectures in many schools and colleges, including London University.

A volunteer for the Dyslexia Association, organising events, talks, games afternoons and other activities for sixteen years. In 2000, Wendy received the Millennium Award for Special Needs Education.

As she had always written poetry, short stories as well as writing things for the children, Wendy decided to concentrate on writing when she retired. She and Jim bought a house in France and moved there permanently in 2007, where she soon met Gordon and Jocelyn Simms, both successful poets. Wendy gained huge benefits from their poetry courses as well as from their encouragement and inspiration.

Gordon submitted Wendy's poem "Letter from a Survivor" to the Segora Open Poetry Competition in 2011, which received a "Highly Commended" and is due to be included in the accompanying anthology.